fold it
calm

fold it
calm

Simple origami to quieten your mind

LI KIM GOH

EBURY
PRESS

contents

Projects

Introduction

My story

I've loved origami my whole life. Growing up, I didn't have lots of toys or games. I was one of four children, and we made do with what we had, often just coloured pencils and paper. One of my earliest memories is creating a paper *sampan* boat, a paper toy that my mother taught me to make, which even floated on water. It has a roof on one side, and as a child, I liked to make two large ones to wear on my feet like a pair of slippers. I also used them to store my pencils and stationery on my desk.

I have many wonderful childhood memories associated with origami. Every weekend we had a family day when my parents would take us swimming, for a picnic or to the cinema. We didn't own a car, so we would take public transport to get there, then keep all of the tickets and fold them into something special. As a family of six, we had lots of tickets to use and we made many things. I found it so much fun to create these toys with my siblings. One of the highlights was a helicopter which could fly, spinning as it gently floated down. It's one of the coolest things you can make out of a bus ticket. It amazed me that a flat sheet of paper could turn into something completely different with just a few simple folds. I'm still fascinated by it and will always be.

Growing my audience

It was only recently that I began to share my love of origami with a wider audience. During the 2020 pandemic, my husband suggested I start uploading origami videos to TikTok. At first I wasn't sure – thinking TikTok was mostly for dance videos – but I liked the idea of being able to share my work to provide entertainment for others. I had previously uploaded some printable projects to my blog, but stopped when work became too busy. Now, with extra time on my hands, I began to share videos of me folding to TikTok, usually with some music in the background. I was surprised when I saw my following growing quickly. It was lovely to have people liking and commenting on my work, and requesting to see different creations. This motivated me to keep going.

I try to choose simple tutorials to share, always ending up with a video that is less than 60 seconds long. In that one minute I aim to fit in every stage of folding, unfolding and paper creasing, all of which are important details. When I looked at other papercraft or origami videos on TikTok, I noticed that most of them do not show the whole process, so this was important to me.

Fold it calm

It seems that people find my origami soothing to watch as I do to create it. For me, origami is fun and relaxing, a good reason to stay away from the computer and do something with my hands. It gives me a sense of satisfaction to fold and crease the paper precisely, and to create beautiful little objects. Just like knitting, drawing, painting and gardening, which all give me a sense of calmness and relaxation, my mind is free from thoughts and stress when I do origami.

I have always enjoyed the peace that I find when folding; it keeps me in the moment and gives me a way to express my creativity. I enjoy challenging myself with a new project, and the sense of accomplishment that comes from completing it. Origami has taught me to be patient, and even when folding a difficult model I never get frustrated. I have been told I should try meditating as I have so much patience from origami!

I hope you will find that sense of calm as you work through this book. Each of these projects should give you 5-10 minutes of mindful relaxation. Some are classics, some are my own creations and they are all suitable for beginners, selected for their practicality, as well as their beauty.

Origami basics

Each project is accompanied by step-by-step diagrams, based on the easy-to-follow Yoshizawa-Randlett system. Where it is hard to demonstrate in 2D, I have included a 3D view.

On the following pages are the symbols, types of folds and basic bases that you will need to understand and learn before starting origami. Refer to these pages anytime you are lost. Once you have learned the basics, you will be able to read and successfully fold any model with diagram instructions, not just in this book, without needing to find 'how to fold' YouTube videos. To me, this is the proper way to learn origami: being able to read and understand the diagram, almost like understanding a maths formula, but much simpler!

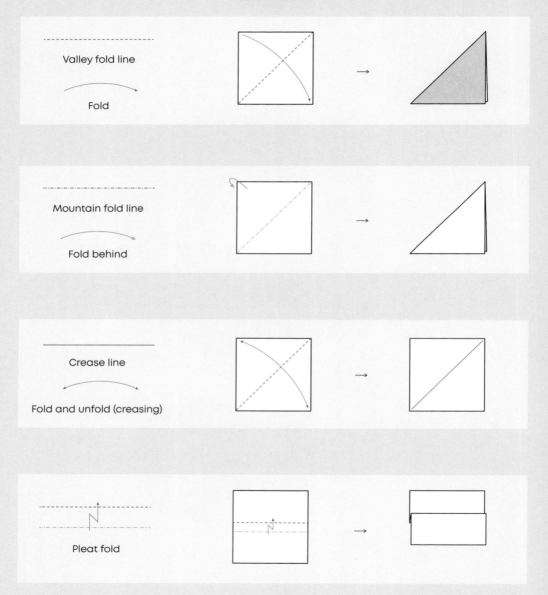

Valley fold line

Fold

Mountain fold line

Fold behind

Crease line

Fold and unfold (creasing)

Pleat fold

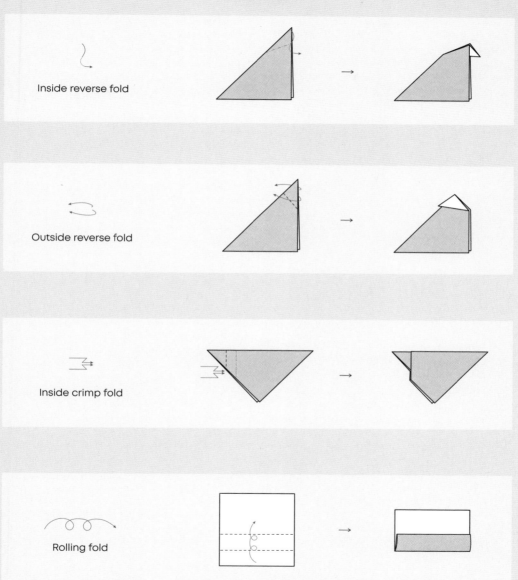

Inside reverse fold

Outside reverse fold

Inside crimp fold

Rolling fold

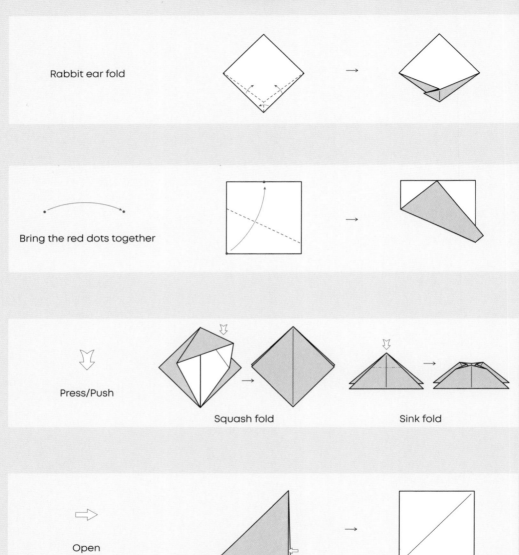

Rabbit ear fold

Bring the red dots together

Press/Push

Squash fold

Sink fold

Open

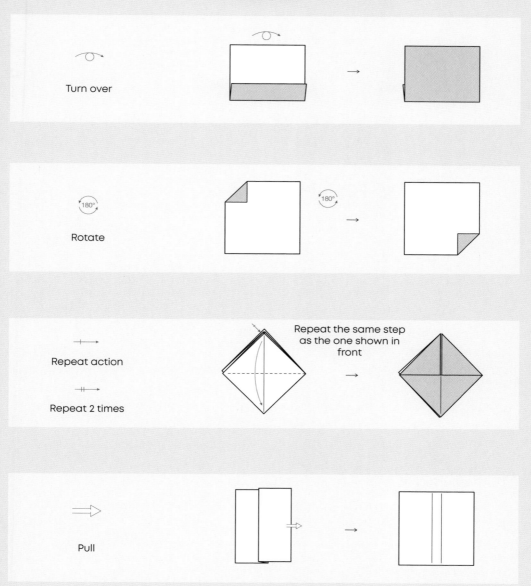

Turn over

Rotate

Repeat action

Repeat 2 times

Repeat the same step as the one shown in front

Pull

Basic bases

Origami bases are the foundation and starting point for many of the origami models. A base is a sequence of basic folds used at the beginning of a model and you will find many of the origami models share the same base at the start. The two most common basic bases, the preliminary and waterbomb bases, are used very often, especially for the traditional models. I have included the base diagrams that are used for the models in this book: preliminary base, waterbomb base, kite base, diamond base, blintz base, bird base, boat base and frog base. You will also learn squash fold when folding the preliminary base and waterbomb base, and petal fold when folding the bird base and frog base. Once you master these bases you are able to fold most of the traditional models, and even develop your own origami creations using them.

Preliminary base

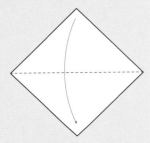

1. Holding the paper like a diamond, fold the paper in half, top to bottom.

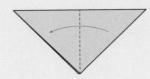

2. Fold the triangle in half, bringing the right corner to meet the left corner.

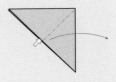

3. Lift the top layer and bring to the right.

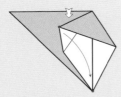

4. Bring the red dots together, lining up the crease line and the centre. Press down to flatten into a diamond with a squash fold.

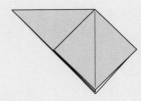

5. Turn over.

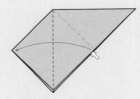

6. Lift the top layer and bring to the left.

7. Bring the red dots together, lining up the crease line and the centre. Press down to flatten into a diamond with a squash fold.

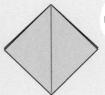

Preliminary base created!

Waterbomb base

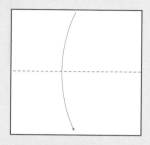

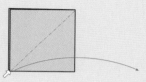

1. Fold the top edge down to meet the bottom.

2. Fold in half, bringing right side to meet left side.

3. Lift the top layer and bring the corner to the right.

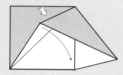

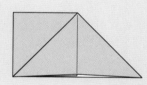

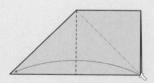

4. Line up the crease line and the centre. Press down to flatten into a triangle with a squash fold.

5. Turn over.

6. Lift the top layer and bring the corner to the left.

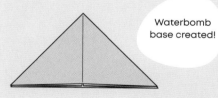

Waterbomb base created!

7. Line up the crease line and the centre. Press down to flatten into a triangle with a squash fold.

Kite base

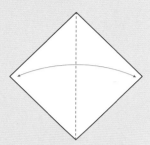 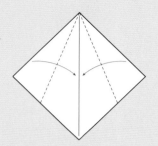 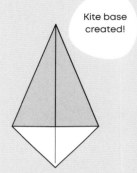

Kite base created!

1 Holding the paper like a diamond, fold the paper in half vertically. Unfold.

2 Fold the top edges to the centre.

Diamond base

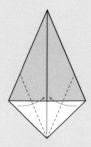 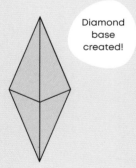

Diamond base created!

1 Make a kite base. Fold the bottom edges to the centre.

Blintz base

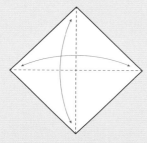

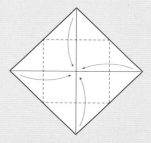

1. Holding the paper like a diamond, fold and unfold the paper horizontally and vertically.

2. Fold all corners to the centre.

Blintz base created!

Bird base

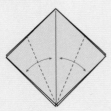

1. Make a preliminary base (see page 20). Fold the bottom edges (just the top flaps) to the centre. Unfold.

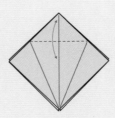

2. Fold down the top to the centre (above the creases from step 1). Unfold.

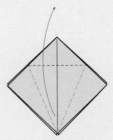

3. Bring the bottom point up.

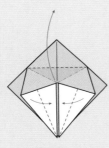

4. As you lift the top layer, fold the sides in to the centre.

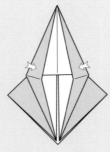

5. Press down and flatten and create a petal fold.

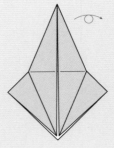

6. Turn over.

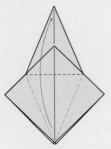

7. Repeat steps 1–5 to create another petal fold.

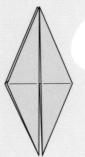

Bird base created!

Boat base

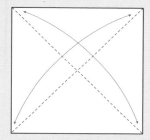

1. Fold and unfold the paper on both diagonals.

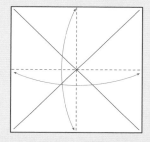

2. Fold and unfold the paper horizontally and vertically.

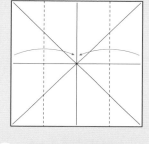

3. Fold the side edges to the centre.

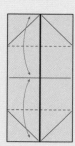

4. Fold the top and bottom edges to the centre. Unfold.

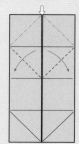

5. Open the top half and fold on the lines shown.

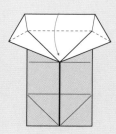

6. Fold the top down and flatten.

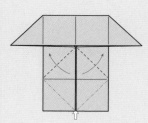

7. Open the bottom half, fold on the lines shown.

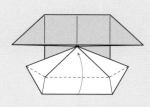

8. Fold the bottom up and flatten.

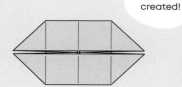

Boat base created!

Frog base

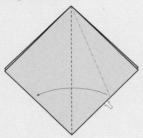

1. Make a preliminary base (see page 20). Bring the top right layer to the left.

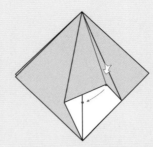

2. Line up the crease line and the centre, press down to flatten with a squash fold.

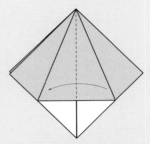

3. Fold the top right flap to the left.

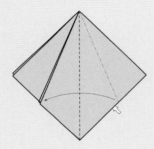

4. Take the right top layer and lift to the left.

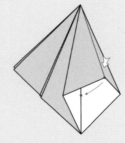

5. Repeat step 2.

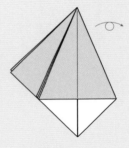

6. Turn over.

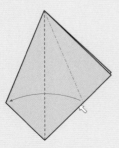

7. Take the right top layer and lift it to the left.

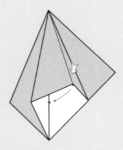

8. Repeat step 2.

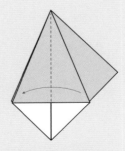

9. Fold the top right flap to the left.

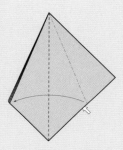

10 Take the top right layer and lift to the left.

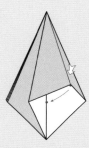

11 Repeat step 2.

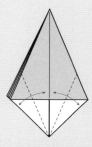

12 Fold the bottom edges (just the top flaps) to the centre. Unfold.

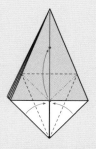

13 Lift the centre up and fold the sides in to the centre.

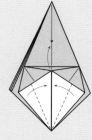

14 Flatten, bringing the red dots together to complete the petal fold.

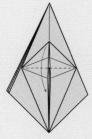

15 Fold the triangle flap down.

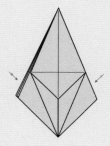

16 Repeat steps 12-15 on the other three sides.

Frog base created!

projects

Sailboat

This traditional origami sailboat is cute, fun and easy to make for all ages. It's perfect for beginners and a great model to learn the inside reverse fold technique. It has two sails that show the opposite side of the paper. It is free-standing (fold down the triangle at the back to help it stand) and has multiple pockets for inserting a notecard, so is perfect to use as a table place card. They are sweet little decorations for kids' rooms or parties. You can arrange them on a string to make a garland or use on a greetings card for Father's day or as a gift tag.

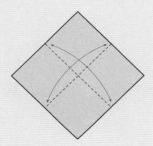

1 Fold and unfold the paper in half.

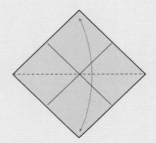

2 Fold the paper in half. Unfold.

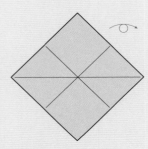

3 Turn over.

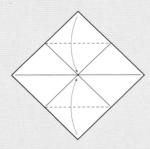

4 Fold the top and bottom corners to the centre.

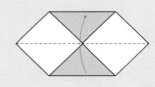

5 Fold the bottom up to the top edge.

6 Inside reverse fold both sides.

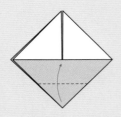

7 Fold the bottom corner up to the centre.

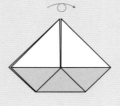

8 Turn over.

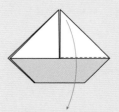

9 Fold down the right triangle flap.

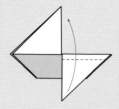 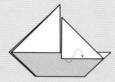 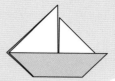

10 Fold the triangle flap up on the line shown.

11 Tuck the bottom of the triangle inside the pocket at the base of the boat.

Your sailboat is complete!

Picture frame

This inexpensive, decorative picture frame makes a cute display to show off your favourite photo, drawing or your favourite quote, and it also makes a perfect gift. It is based on the boat base. Add a magnet on the back to display on your refrigerator, use it as a fancy gift tag or fold it using pretty decorative paper to match your room. You can connect them easily to make double photo frames or accordion frames that can stand on their own. When folded from a 15cm square piece of paper, it will hold a 7x7cm photo, making it a nice little pocket-size frame.

Base used: boat (page 25)

You, me
and
the dog

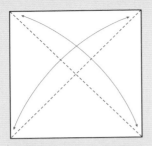

1   Fold and unfold the paper.

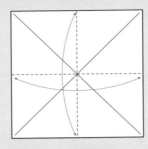

2   Fold and unfold the paper.

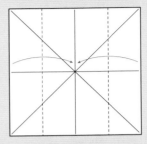

3   Fold the side edges to the centre.

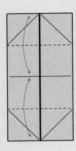

4   Fold the top and bottom edges to the centre. Unfold.

5   Open the top half and fold on the lines shown.

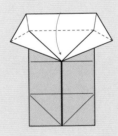

6   Fold the top down and flatten it.

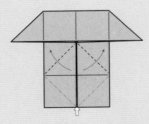

7   Open the bottom half and fold on the lines shown.

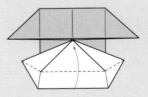

8   Fold the bottom up and flatten into a boat base.

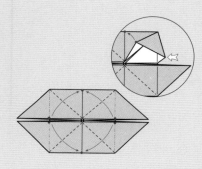

9. Create valley folds on the lines shown, then bring the red dots together and squash fold on all four points.

10. Fold the inside corners to meet the outer corners.

11. Lift the top layer of each corner and fold in so the point meets the fold from step 10.

12. Fold all corners of the smaller triangles as shown.

Your picture frame is complete! Turn the page to continue.

TO JOIN PICTURE FRAMES

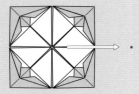

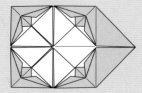

13 Lift the triangle flap beneath out and flatten.

14 The picture frame now has a triangle flap pointing to the right.

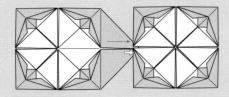

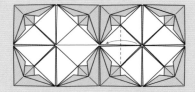

15 Insert the triangle flap inside the left pocket on the second picture frame.

16 Fold the diamond shape in half to lock the frames together.

Double picture frame completed!

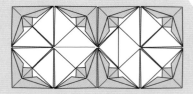

Join as many as you want to make accordion frames.

Heart place card

Impress your guests with this romantic heart-shaped place card I created. The paper heart has two pockets for placing the card, one on the back and one on the front. When folded with a 15cm square piece of paper, a 6x5cm notecard fits in the back pocket and a 6x2cm one fits in the front pocket. The simple and stylish design makes it a welcoming table setting for special banquets, family reunions, birthday parties and intimate receptions. Choose your favourite paper to complement the theme or the occasion's style and ambience. This model is multifunctional, your guests can take it home as a favour and use it as a bookmark.

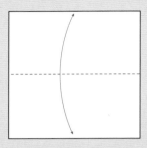

1 Fold the paper in half. Unfold.

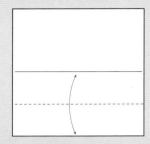

2 Fold the bottom edge to the centre. Unfold.

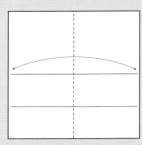

3 Fold the paper in half. Unfold.

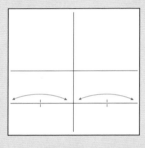

4 Fold the sides to the centre, make a small crease on the bottom fold. Unfold.

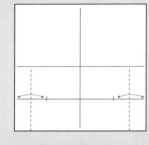

5 Fold the sides to the crease you just made, crease only on the lines as shown on the bottom half. Unfold.

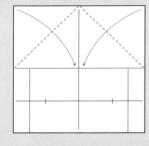

6 Fold the top corners down to the centre.

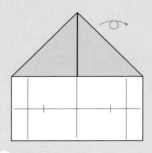

7 Turn over.

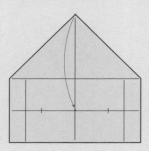

8 Fold the top point down to meet the red dot.

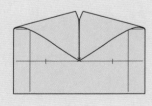

9 Hold the point you just folded down in place (marked x). Turn over.

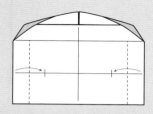

10   Fold the sides in to the creases made in step 4 and flatten.

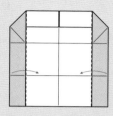

11   Fold the sides in as shown.

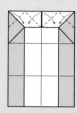

12   Fold the top corners down to create two triangles.

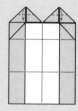

13   Fold top points down.

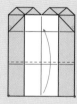

14   Fold the bottom edge up and tuck corners just inside the triangle pockets (bringing the red dots to the red dashed dots in the diagram).

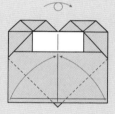

15   Fold bottom corners up.

Your heart place card is complete!

Insert a notecard in the back pocket or the slit in the front.

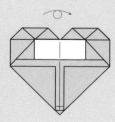

16   Turn over.

Paper balloon

This origami balloon, also known as a waterbomb or water balloon, is a cute traditional model. It is an inflatable paper toy – you can play with it like a ball or fill it with water to make a waterbomb, but you'd better throw it quickly before the paper gets all soggy! It's environmentally friendly and a great alternative to latex rubber water balloons. Besides being a fun paper toy, it's great for home decoration. My favourite decorative use is as fairy light covers, inserting the led lights inside so they are illuminated. It creates a different ambience depending on the design and colour of the paper you use. It also makes a cute hanging ornament. **Base used:** waterbomb (page 21)

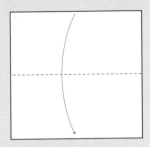

1 Fold the paper in half.

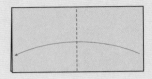

2 Fold the paper in half again.

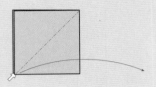

3 Lift the top layer and bring the corner to the right.

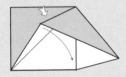

4 Line up the crease line and the centre, press down and squash fold into a triangle.

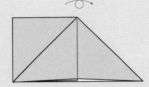

5 Turn over.

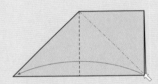

6 Lift the top layer and bring the corner to the left.

7 Line up the crease line and centre, press down and squash fold into a waterbomb base.

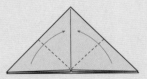

8 Fold the bottom edges (just the top flaps) to the centre.

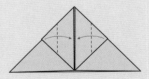

9 Fold the side corners to the centre.

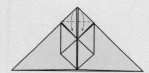

10   Fold the top flaps down.

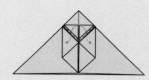

11   Tuck the triangle flaps made in step 10 into the pockets.

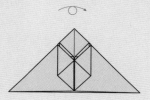

12   Turn over.

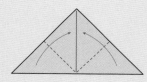

13   Fold the bottom edges to the centre.

14   Fold the side corners to the centre.

15   Fold top flaps down.

16   Tuck the triangle flaps made in step 15 into the pockets.

17   Puff up by blowing air into the hole at the bottom.

Your balloon is complete!

Star

This traditional four-point star model is simple and beautiful. It's not hard to fold if you know how to fold an origami crane (see page 56). It uses the same steps as folding a crane but starts with a blintz base. This model is 3D and looks pretty on both sides. On the layered side, it reveals a bit of the opposite side of the paper, so consider using paper with different colours or patterns on both sides. Hang it on a tree or in a window as an ornament, string it into a garland or use it to adorn your presents. It's an easy, inexpensive, elegant and beautiful decoration for Christmas time. **Bases used:** blintz (page 23) and preliminary (page 20)

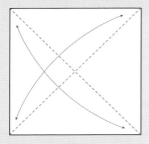

1. Fold and unfold the paper.

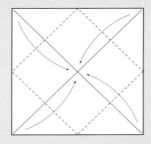

2. Fold all corners to the centre to create a blintz base.

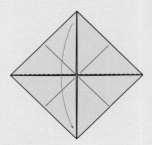

3. Fold down in half.

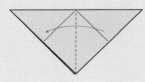

4. Fold the triangle in half.

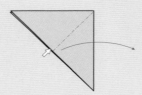

5. Lift the top layer and bring to the right. Squash fold into a diamond shape.

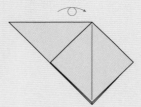

6. Turn over.

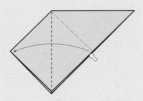

7. Lift the top layer and bring to the left. Squash fold into a preliminary base.

8. Fold bottom edges (just the top flaps) to the centre. Unfold. Fold down the top quarter (above the creases). Unfold.

9. Bring the bottom point (top layer only) up to the top.

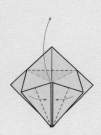

10 While bringing the bottom point up, fold in the sides.

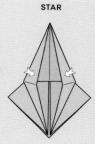

11 Press sides and flatten to create a petal fold.

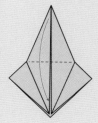

12 Fold the flap down.

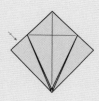

13 Repeat steps 8-12 to create a petal fold on the other side.

14 Rotate 180°.

15 Pull open all four flaps.

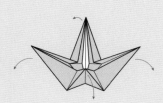

16 Continue to pull open until the inside layer is revealed.

Your star ornament is complete!

Butterfly

There are many ways to fold butterflies – this is the traditional one using a boat base at the start. It's very easy to fold, is great for beginners and produces a simple yet beautiful and delicate result. Use pretty origami paper for this to create fun spring home decor. Stick it on the wall, window or the flower of a plant! It's also ideal for making hanging decorations, as a gift tag or on a greetings card, or just simply a keepsake for someone special.
Base used: boat (page 25)

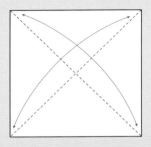

1. Fold and unfold the paper in half.

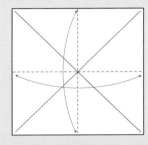

2. Fold and unfold the paper in half.

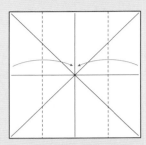

3. Fold the side edges in to the centre.

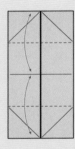

4. Fold the top and bottom edges to the centre. Unfold.

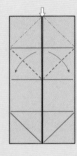

5. Open the top half and fold on the lines shown.

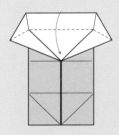

6. Fold the top down and flatten.

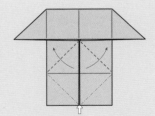

7. Open the bottom half and fold on the lines shown.

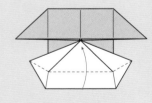

8. Fold the bottom up and flatten into a boat base.

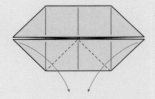

9. Fold bottom flaps down.

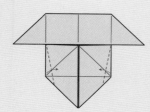

10 Fold corners in at an angle
    as shown.

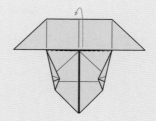

11 Fold top section back.

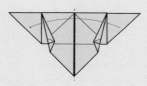

12 Fold in half.

13 Fold back the front and
    back wings at an angle
    as shown.

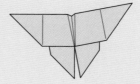

Your butterfly
is complete!

Crane

The origami crane is the most popular traditional model. It's a symbol of peace, good health and longevity. Traditionally, it is believed that folding 1,000 paper cranes (called *senbazuru* in Japanese) gives you one wish. Cranes were believed to live for 1,000 years, so one crane is folded for each year. In some versions of the story, folding *senbazuru* brings a person good luck and happiness. Today, we gift origami cranes as symbols of hope, love, friendship and world peace. This model takes perseverance and patience, but you will be rewarded with a beautiful and intricate final piece. **Bases used:** preliminary (page 20) and bird (page 24)

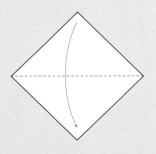

1 Fold the paper in half.

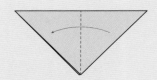

2 Fold the triangle in half.

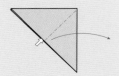

3 Lift the top layer and bring to the right. Line up the crease line and the centre, press down and squash fold into a diamond.

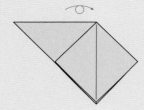

4 Turn over.

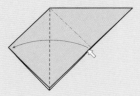

5 Lift the top layer and bring to the left. Line up the crease line and the centre, press down and squash fold into a preliminary base.

6 Fold the bottom edges (just the top flap) to the centre. Unfold. Fold down the top quarter (above the creases from the previous fold). Unfold.

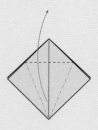

7 Bring the bottom point up.

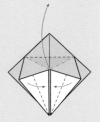

8 While bringing the bottom point up, fold in the sides.

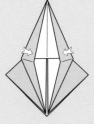

9 Press sides and flatten to create a petal fold.

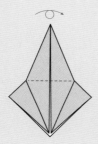

10 Turn over.

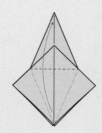

11 Repeat steps 6-9 to create a petal fold on the other side and finish the bird base.

12 Fold bottom edges (just the top flap) to the centre.

13 Turn over.

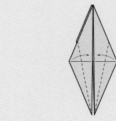

14 Fold bottom edges to the centre.

15 Inside reverse fold the bottom points.

16 Inside reverse fold the left tip to form the head.

17 Spread the wings.

Your crane is complete!

Dove

This origami dove is a traditional model. It's very easy to fold without any complicated folding techniques, but the result is so beautiful and graceful with its angled wings. It's perfect for beginners. The dove represents peace, love, gentleness, freedom and purity which makes it a perfect card embellishment for lots of different occasions.

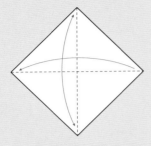

1 Fold the paper down in half. Unfold. Then fold the paper in half, bringing the right corner to the left corner.

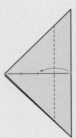

2 Fold the right edge to the middle.

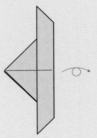

3 Turn over.

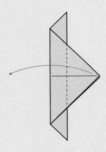

4 Fold the top layer to the left, so the right edge lines up with the edge behind.

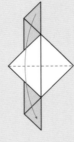

5 Fold down in half.

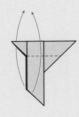

6 Fold both wings up.

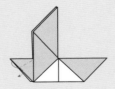

7 Inside reverse fold the left point to make the head.

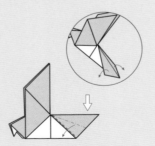

8 Press the right edge down and flatten the tail.

Your dove is complete!

Fox

This fox origami creation of mine is not only adorable with its big 3D ears, but it's also a functional model with many uses. It can be used as a bookmark, a card embellishment, home decor for a woodland-themed party or as a finger puppet for kids. It uses the squash fold for the ears and a rabbit ear fold for the nose. It can be a bit tricky folding the nose because it's quite small. But don't let that discourage you! Origami takes lots of practice, your skill will improve and your projects will get better and better. You can leave the face blank or make your own fox character by drawing eyes.

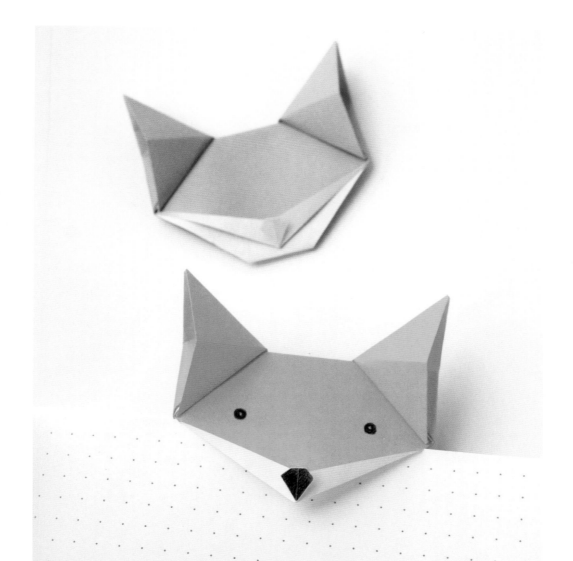

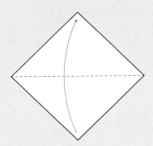

1 Fold the paper in half.

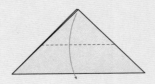

2 Fold both layers of the top point down slightly past the bottom edge.

3 Fold the sides back.

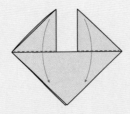

4 Fold top triangles down.

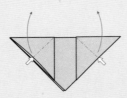

5 Open the top layers and lift up.

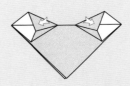

6 Squash fold into a diamond shape.

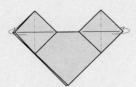
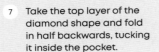

7 Take the top layer of the diamond shape and fold in half backwards, tucking it inside the pocket.

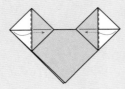

8 Take the bottom flap of the diamond shape and fold in half forwards, tucking it inside the pocket.

9 Taking the top layer only, fold the bottom edges in as shown, then pinch and make a rabbit ear fold.

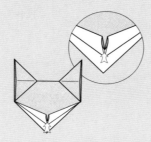

10   Lift the 'rabbit ear' up towards the centre.

11   Squash fold the centre of the 'rabbit ear' down into a flat diamond shape.

12   Fold the top tip of diamond shape behind. Fold the bottom point behind, tucking it inside the layers.

Your fox is complete!

If you want to bring your fox to life, you can draw a nose and eyes.

Penguin

There are many different versions of the origami penguin, some are simple, some are complex. This version is one of my creations and is a simple one. It stands on its own and has a little pocket on both sides to hold a toothpick with a flag, a little card or small items. It's perfect to use as a place card, a cute information sign or a decoration for your desk. It needs to be divided equally in a few places; you can divide it using a ruler or just eyeball it. The markings are there to give you a sense of the distance, but you do not have to follow these precisely. It will still work if you are out by a few millimetres.

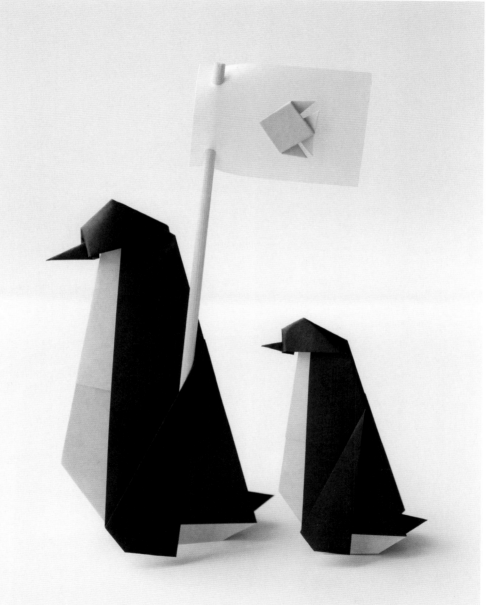

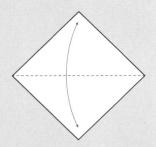

1   Fold the paper in half.
    Unfold.

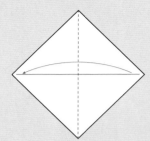

2   Fold the paper in half.

3   Fold the top layer of the left
    corner one-eighth behind.
    Repeat on the layer behind.

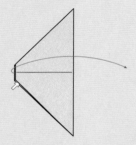

4   Open the paper.

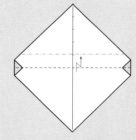

5   Pleat fold the top half down
    one-fifth.

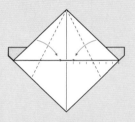

6   Fold the top edges down
    to meet the red dots (about
    one-eighth from the centre).

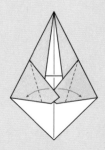

7   Fold the flaps back
    as shown.

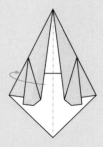

8   Mountain fold in half.

9   Inside reverse fold the
    bottom point.

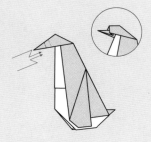

10. Fold the top layer of the bottom point behind. Repeat on the layer behind.

11. Outside reverse fold to create the head.

12. Inside crimp fold to create the beak.

Your penguin is complete!

Camellia with leaf

This beautiful traditional camellia flower is tricky to fold using an asymmetric squash fold. It can be a bit challenging for a beginner, so I would suggest you try this project after you have perfected some of the simpler ones. But once you are familiar with it, and understand the asymmetric squash fold, it gets easier and fun to fold because you are basically doing the same step four times. Use the camellia flower as a table decoration or on a card or gift wrapping. Nest them into one another using different size pieces of paper: reduce the size by 4cm for each nested flower (see an example of this on page 13). The leaf is a very easy-to-fold traditional model and nicely complements the flower.

CAMELLIA FLOWER

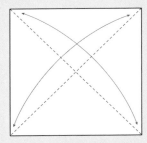

1 Fold and unfold the paper in half.

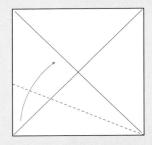

2 Fold the bottom edge to the centre (this is a half kite fold).

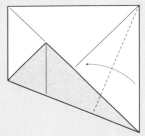

3 Fold the right edge to the centre.

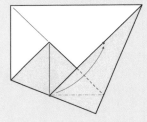

4 Lift the corner with the red dot to meet the other red dot, creating a valley fold on the line shown.

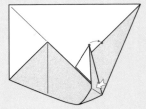

5 Notice how the paper curves up. Line up the straight edge when putting the red dots together, press down to flatten with an asymmetric squash fold.

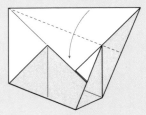

6 Fold the top edge to the centre.

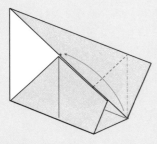

7 Lift the corner with the red dot to meet the other red dot, creating a valley fold on the line shown. This is the same as step 4.

8 Notice how the paper curves up. Line up the straight edge when putting the red dots together, press down to flatten with an asymmetric squash fold. This is the same as step 5.

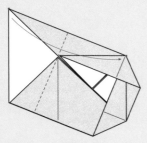

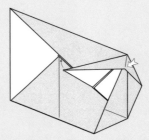

9 Fold the left edge to the centre. It is hard to see where the centre is, so use the red dots as a guide. Line up the top edges.

10 Lift the corner with the red dot to meet the other red dot, creating a valley fold on the line shown. This is the same as steps 4 and 7.

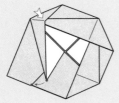

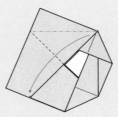

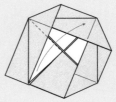

11 Notice how the paper curves up again. Line up the edge when putting the red dots together, press down to flatten with an asymmetric squash fold.

12 Fold the flap up on the existing crease line.

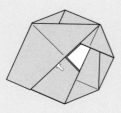

13 Open the flap but not all the way.

14 Pull the paper beneath out as much as you can.

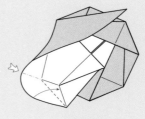

15 Here you will see the existing crease lines. Invert the highlighted creases.

16 Close the flap back and flatten.

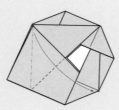

17 Lift the corner with the red dot to meet the other red dot, creating a valley fold on the line shown. This is the same as steps 4, 7 and 10.

18 One last time the paper will curve up. Line up the edge when putting the red dots together, press down to flatten with an asymmetric squash fold.

19 Fold the flap down and tuck it inside the pocket.

20 Tuck in the last corner inside the pocket.

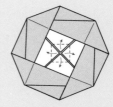

21 Fold all four corners out.

LEAF

22 Use a piece of paper half the size you used for the camellia. Start by folding the paper in half.

23 Pleat fold into quarters.

24 Pull open.

25 On the diagonal edge, fold in an angle as shown.

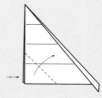

26 Fold the top layer of the corner up. Fold the bottom layer back.

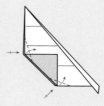

27 Fold the corners of the top layer as shown to soften the edge. Repeat for the bottom layer.

28 Open the leaf.

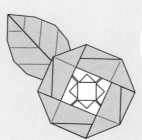

Place the flower onto the leaf and it is complete!

Lily

The origami lily, also known as the iris, is a well-loved traditional origami flower because of its almost lifelike beautiful petals and stamens. Familiarise yourself with the frog base and you are pretty close to creating this beautiful flower with just a few more steps added after that. Use different sizes and different colour paper to create a beautiful display, perfect for table centrepieces, or add stems to create a beautiful paper bouquet. **Bases used:** preliminary (page 20) and frog (page 26)

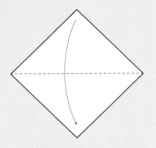

1. Fold the paper in half.

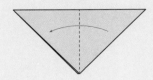

2. Fold the triangle in half.

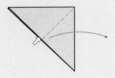

3. Lift the top layer and bring to the right.

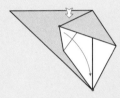

4. Line up the crease line and the centre, press down and squash fold into a diamond.

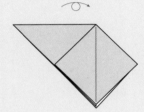

5. Turn over.

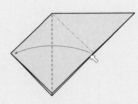

6. Lift the top layer and bring to the left.

7. Line up the crease line and the centre, press down and squash fold into a preliminary base.

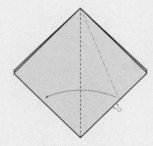

8. Bring the right top layer to the left.

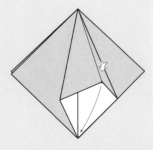

9. Line up the crease line and the centre, press down and squash fold.

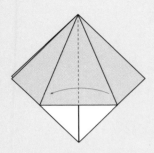

10   Fold the top right flap to the left.

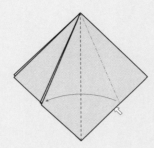

11   Take the right layer and lift it to the left.

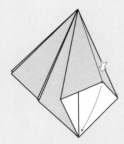

12   Line up the crease line and the centre, press down and squash fold.

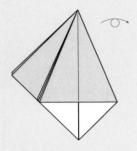

13   Turn over.

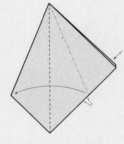

14   Repeat steps 8-12 on the other side.

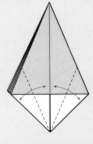

15   Fold the bottom edges (just the top flaps) to the centre. Unfold.

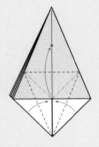

16   Lift the centre flap up and fold the sides in to the centre.

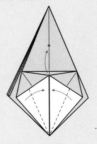

17   Flatten to bring the red dots together to complete the petal fold.

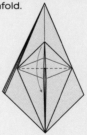

18   Fold the triangle flap down.

19 Repeat steps 15-18 on the other three sides to create a frog base.

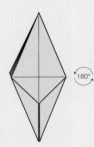

20 Rotate 180°.

21 Fold the top left flap to the right.

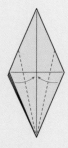

22 Fold the bottom edges (just the top flaps) to the centre.

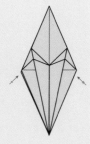

23 Repeat steps 21 and 22 on the other three sides.

24 Fold down the top points to create the petals.

Your lily is complete!

Optional
Use a pencil to curl the petals for a softer effect.

Potted cactus

This cute cactus is another one of my creations, folded with two pieces of paper the same size. The cactus is based on a bird base. If you can fold an origami crane, you will have no problem with this. The one new fold technique that is introduced in this model is the sink fold, which is a standard fold in origami but is considered advanced. The cactus is one of the coolest houseplants and is a stylish design for crafts, home decors and prints because of its funny and distinct appearance. Have fun folding these cute cacti, they can stand on their own to display, or can stay flat for embellishing cards or even as a framed art piece.

Bases used: preliminary (page 20) and bird (page 24)

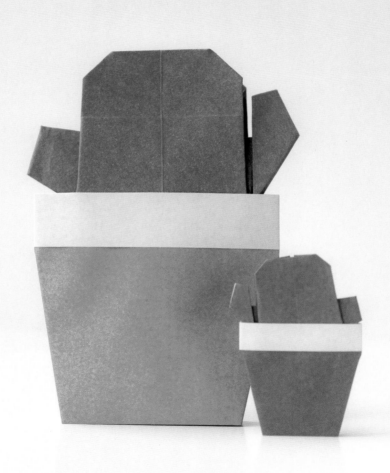

CACTUS

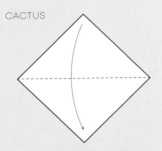

1 Fold the paper in half.

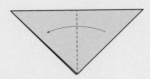

2 Fold the triangle in half.

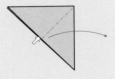

3 Lift the top layer and bring to the right. Squash fold into a diamond.

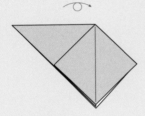

4 Turn over.

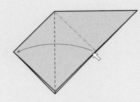

5 Lift the top layer and bring to the left. Squash fold into a preliminary base.

6 Fold the bottom edges (just the top flap) and top to the centre. Unfold.

7 Bring the bottom point up.

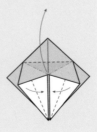

8 Fold the sides in to the centre.

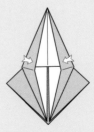

9 Press the sides down and flatten to create a petal fold.

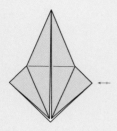

10 Repeat steps 6-9 to create a petal fold on the other side and finish the bird base.

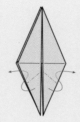

11 Inside reverse fold the bottom flaps on the lines indicated.

12 Inside reverse fold the left point on the line indicated. Outside reverse fold the tip of the right point.

13 Outside reverse fold the right arm. Fold in between the flaps.

14 Bring the top flap down. Repeat on the other side.

15 Fold down the top point. Unfold.

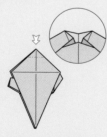

16 Press the top point down into an open sink fold.

17 Fold the top layer of the sides back. Repeat on the other side.

Your cactus is complete! Turn the page to continue.

POT

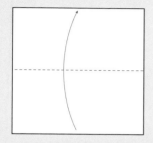

18   Fold the paper up in half.

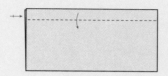

19   Fold the top layer down. Repeat on the layer behind.

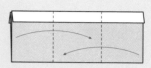

20   Fold the sides into thirds on the lines shown.

21   Tuck the right flap in the pocket of the left flap.

22   Tuck the top flap under the top flap of the layer behind.

23   Inside reverse fold the sides as shown.

24   Turn over your complete pot.

25   Insert cactus inside the front pocket.

Your potted cactus is complete!

Tulip

This traditional tulip flower model can be both 3D and free-standing for display or lie flat to be used on cards, especially for Mother's Day. They are perfect for beautiful spring decoration and look lovely when bunched together. It's relatively easy to fold, and a fun project for beginners and all ages. **Bases used:** waterbomb (page 21), kite (page 22) and diamond (page 22)

TULIP FLOWER

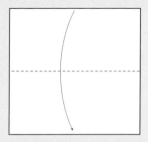

1　Fold the paper in half.

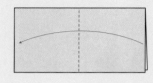

2　Fold the paper in half again.

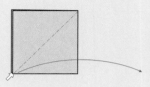

3　Lift the top layer and bring the corner to the right.

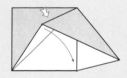

4　Line up the crease line and the centre, press down and squash fold into a triangle.

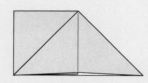

5　Turn over.

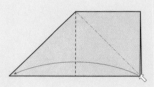

6　Lift the top layer and bring the corner to the left.

7　Line up the crease line and the centre, press down and squash fold into a waterbomb base .

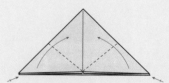

8　Lifting the top flaps, fold the corners up not quite to the centre. Repeat on the other side.

9　Lift the top layer and fold behind the sides on the lines shown. Repeat on the other side to complete your tulip flower.

STEM

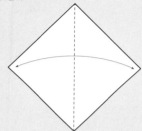

10 Fold the paper in half. Unfold.

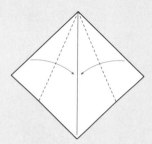

11 Fold the top edges to the centre to create a kite base.

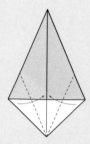

12 Fold the bottom edges to the centre to create a diamond base.

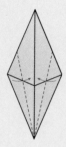

13 Fold the bottom edges to the centre.

14 Fold up on the line shown.

15 Fold in half.

16 Pull the top tip away from the outer flap slightly.

17 Outside reverse fold the outer layer.

Your tulip is complete!

18 Insert the tip of the stem inside the small opening at the bottom of the tulip.

Fir tree

This model is one of my creations. It's a *kirigami*, a variation of origami that involves cutting and folding. It's very easy to make and a great activity for all ages during the festive season. Start with a preliminary base and continue as if to create a frog base but without making the petal folds. Its simple and clean design makes it perfect to use on any Christmas table setting, and you can turn it into a place card holder by cutting a slit on the tip. It can be used for a pop-up Christmas card, on gift wrapping or as an ornament, paper garland or even a centrepiece, if you fold many in different sizes using pretty paper. **Base used:** preliminary (page 20)

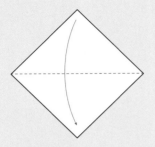

1. Fold the paper in half.

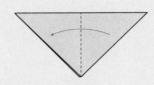

2. Fold the triangle in half.

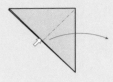

3. Lift the top layer and bring to the right.

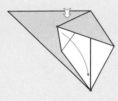

4. Line up the crease line and the centre, press down and squash fold into a diamond.

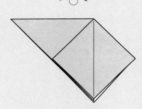

5. Turn over.

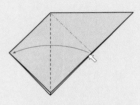

6. Lift the top layer and bring to the left.

7. Line up the crease line and the centre, press down and squash fold into a preliminary base.

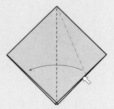

8. Lift the top right layer to the left and squash fold.

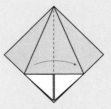

9. Fold the top left flap to the right.

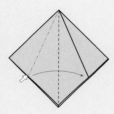

10 Lift the top left layer to the right and squash fold.

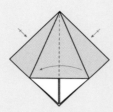

11 Fold the top right flap to the left. Repeat steps 8-11 on the other side.

12 Fold up the top layer of the bottom triangle. Unfold.

13 Cut the triangle in half.

14 Fold the just-cut triangles back to hold the flaps behind together.

15 Repeat steps 12-14 on all the triangle flaps.

Your fir tree is complete!

Masu box

This classic square box is one of my absolute favourite models to fold and I think it's one of the must-learn models for everyone. It only takes a few simple steps to fold and you can easily adapt it to make different sizes. It's a useful, practical box that can be used for just about anything. You can use the masu box as an open container to organise your drawers or shelves. Place your masu box on top of the cube box to create a beautiful gift box with a lid, made extra special by adding a bow or by folding from pretty gift wrapping paper. If you are going to make a bigger box, make sure to use heavier paper so it's sturdy and durable.
Base used: blintz (page 23)

CUBE BOX

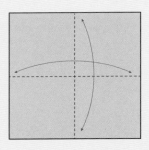

1. Fold and unfold the paper in half.

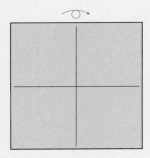

2. Turn over.

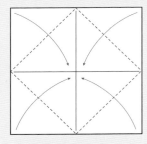

3. Fold corners to the centre to create a blintz base.

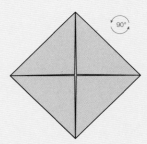

4. Rotate 90°.

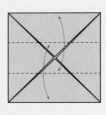

5. Fold into thirds horizontally. Unfold.

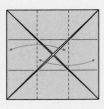

6. Fold into thirds vertically. Unfold.

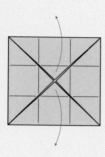

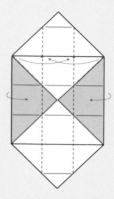

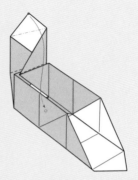

7 Open the top and bottom triangle flaps.

8 Bring the sides up. Bring the red dots together, turning the diagonal folds into mountain folds as you do.

9 Fold the flap down, bringing the red dots together inside the box.

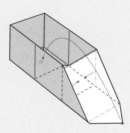

The base of your box is complete! Turn the page to continue.

10 Repeat steps 8-9, on the opposite side.

MASU BOX

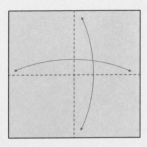

11 Fold and unfold the paper in half.

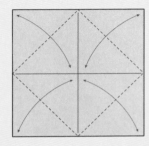

12 Fold the corners to the centre. Unfold.

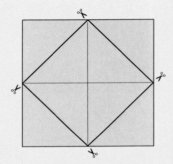

13 Trim on the crease lines you just made with scissors.

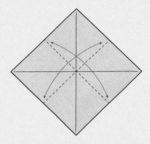

14 Fold and unfold the paper in half.

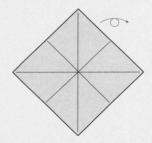

15 Turn over.

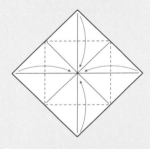

16 Fold the corners to the centre to create a blintz base.

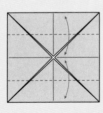

17 Fold the top and bottom edges to the centre. Unfold.

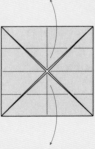

18 Open the top and bottom triangle flaps.

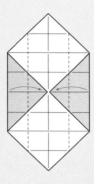

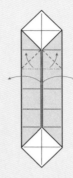

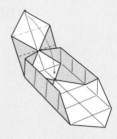

19 Fold the side edges to the centre.

20 Open the centre to the sides and fold on the lines shown to form a box.

21 Fold the flap down, bringing the red dots together inside the box.

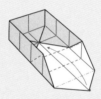

Your masu box is complete!

22 Repeat steps 20-21 on the opposite side.

Twist box

Use the simplest folds to create a unique, elegant and interesting final piece. I like the timeless look and style of this box the best and it's also very satisfying to fold. This pretty twist box has a square base and offset/ twisted square opening, with four repeat triangle patterns on the side. Because it has such a unique look, I like to fold it with very beautiful Washi paper to use as a home decor piece, filling it with some dried flowers, potpourri, shells and rocks collected from my beach holiday. It's also a great little bowl to keep my everyday jewellery in. You can even use it as a key tray, folding from a bigger and heavier-weight paper.

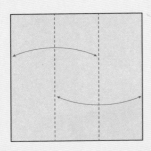

1. Fold into thirds vertically. Unfold.

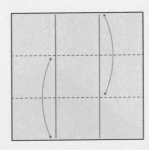

2. Fold into thirds horizontally. Unfold.

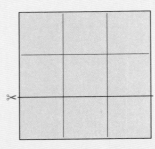

3. Trim off the bottom third with scissors.

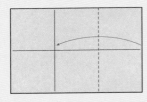

4. Fold the right edge to the first third crease line.

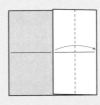

5. Take the left edge of the flap you just made and fold it to the right edge.

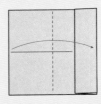

6. Fold in half, bringing the left edge to meet the right edge.

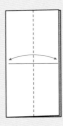

7. Fold the top layer in half, bringing the right edge of the top layer to the left edge. Unfold.

8. Fold the corners in as shown, only lifting the top flap on the right.

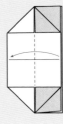

9. Fold the top right flap to the left.

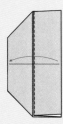

10 Fold the top right layer to the left.

11 Fold all of the corners in as shown.

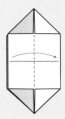

12 Fold the top left flap to the right.

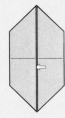

13 Open from the middle.

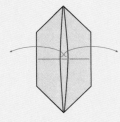

14 Gently pull open the sides.

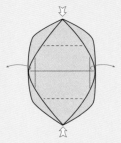

15 Pull left and right sides all the way out while pressing the top and bottom sides down. Flatten down into a 'lips' shape.

16 Release and push the left and right sides to shape into a box.

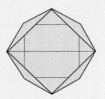

Your twist box is complete!

Sweet box

This classic sweet box not only looks cute, it's also a very practical and useful model, and is very steady with its wider base. It is folded from the preliminary base and with a few more simple steps you have the perfect little box for your sweets and snacks. Choose a beautiful paper to make this with, as the pattern shows on both the inside and outside of the box. It's so easy to make, you can make lots of them in no time for party events and impress your guests by serving snacks in them. It's great for storing other small things too, not just sweets. **Base used:** preliminary (page 20)

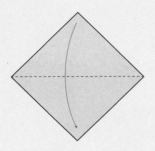

1 Fold the paper in half.

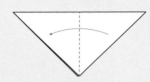

2 Fold the triangle in half.

3 Lift the top layer and bring to the right.

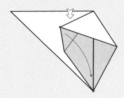

4 Line up the crease line and the centre. Press down and squash fold into a diamond.

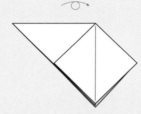

5 Turn over.

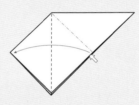

6 Repeat steps 3-4, lifting the top layer to the left to make a preliminary base.

7 Rotate 180°.

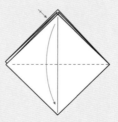

8 Fold the top layer down to the bottom corner. Repeat on the other side.

9 Take the top layer and fold the top edges back towards the centre. Repeat on the other side.

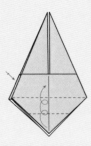

10   Take the top layer and roll fold up. Repeat on the other side.

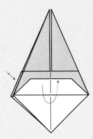

11   Bring the flap down then fold under, tucking it inside the pocket. Repeat on the other side.

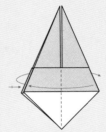

12   Bring the right flap (just the top layer) to the left. Repeat on the other side.

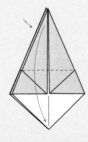

13   Fold the top flap down to the bottom point. Repeat on the other side.

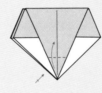

14   Fold the tip up. Repeat on the other side.

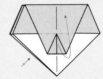

15   Fold the flap behind, tucking it inside the pocket. Repeat on the other side.

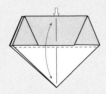

16   Fold the bottom triangle up and unfold. Open the straight edge.

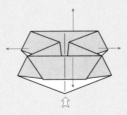

17   Gently pull open the straight edges. Press the bottom up to shape into a box.

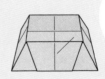

Your sweet box is complete!

Rectangle box

This rearrangement of a classic model makes
a lovely organiser for your home office. It is perfect
to use on the desk or inside drawers. Both sides of
the paper show on the outside of this box. In the
instructions on the next page it is folded from a square
piece of paper. You can fold it with a rectangular piece
of paper using the exact same technique to create
a longer box, which is ideal to use as a pen case.
It can be used as a lid as well, just make sure you
use a slightly bigger piece of paper than the one
you use for the base so it will close properly.

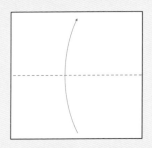

1. Fold the paper in half.

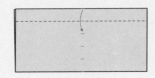

2. Fold both layers of the top edge down one-fifth.

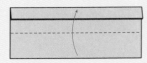

3. Fold the bottom edge to the top edge. Unfold.

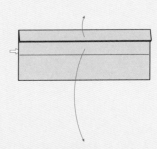

4. Open all folds.

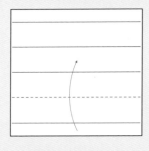

5. You will see the five crease lines you just made. Fold up the bottom edge, turning the second crease line from the bottom into a valley fold.

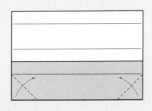

6. Fold the bottom corners to the crease line as shown.

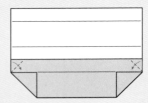

7. Fold the small corners down.

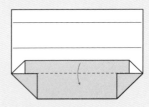

8. Fold the flap down.

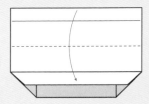

9. Fold down the top edge on the second crease line from the top.

10 Fold the top corners down to the crease line.

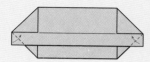

11 Fold the small corners up.

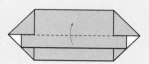

12 Fold the flap up.

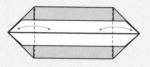

13 Fold the side corners into triangles as shown. Unfold.

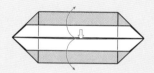

14 Open from the middle.

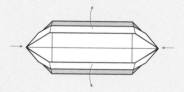

15 Gently pull open the sides and shape into a box.

Your rectangle box is complete!

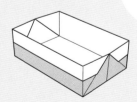

Tato flat box

Tato is a traditional Japanese flat box or pouch. Most self-close and are used to store small and flat objects. What I like about this box is it's collapsible. You can fold lots of them and stack them up without taking up too much space, and open them into a box when ready to use. My mother used to fold these from magazine pages and use them as a place to put food waste. I like to use it to store flat or small presents. It's relatively simple to make, and with a few extra steps, you can make the opening flaps into a heart shape, which is perfect for party or wedding favours.

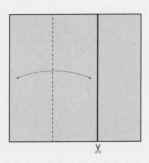

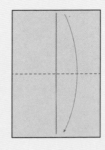

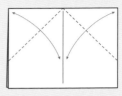

1. Divide paper into thirds and trim off one-third with scissors.

2. Fold the paper in half.

3. Fold the top corners to the centre. Unfold.

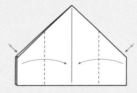

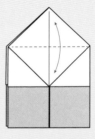

4. Inside reverse fold the top corners.

5. Fold the side edges to the centre (just the top layer). Repeat on the other side.

6. Fold top point to the centre. Unfold.

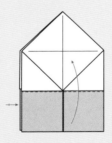

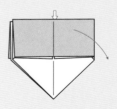

7. Fold the bottom up (just the top layer). Repeat on the other side.

8. Rotate 180°.

9. Open up the straight edge.

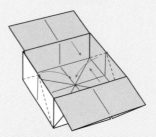

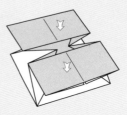

10 Gently pull it open into a box shape.

11 Bring the inside edges of the flaps inwards, folding the sides so the red dots meet.

12 Gently press on top of the box to flatten.

CREATE A BAR DESIGN

Your box with bar design is complete!

13a Fold the flaps in half, tucking underneath.

CREATE A HEART DESIGN

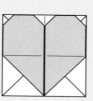

Your box with heart design is complete!

13b Fold the four outside corners back as shown and inside reverse fold the two inside top corners.

Tato envelope

This traditional Japanese self-closing envelope is one of the most practical models to learn. It's a very simple piece to fold, basically just repeatedly overlapping the four flaps and tucking them into one another. With a few extra folds on the flaps you can create a pretty pattern on the top, like this pinwheel tato. You can slightly alter the way it's folded (see step 4) to create different patterns. It's ideal to use paper with a different colour or pattern on each side because both sides are revealed on the top. This tato envelope is perfect for special events and holidays. You can put a banknote inside or use it to wrap cards, gift cards or any small flat items.

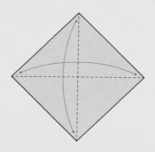

1 Fold and unfold the paper in half.

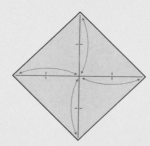

2 Bring the corners to the centre, make a small crease on the dotted lines as shown. Unfold.

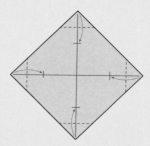

3 Fold the corners to the small crease lines you just made.

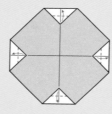

4 Fold the triangle points out to the edge (you can choose to skip this step or fold the triangle behind to get different patterns, see completed pictures).

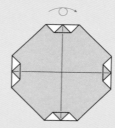

5 Turn over.

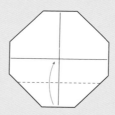

6 Fold the bottom edge to the centre.

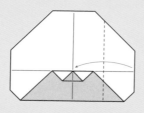

7 Fold the right edge to the centre.

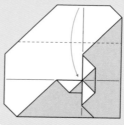

8 Fold the top edge to the centre.

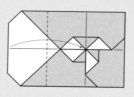

9 Fold the left edge to the centre.

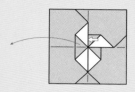

10   Open the left flap.

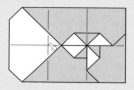

11   Slightly open the left part of the bottom flap (not all the way, just enough to tuck the left flap in).

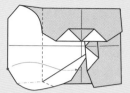

12   Tuck the lower part of the left flap under.

13   Close and flatten.

Your tato envelope is complete!

CREATE A DIFFERENT PATTERN

14a   Create this pattern on the top by folding the triangle point behind in step 4.

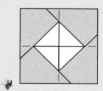

14b   Create this pattern on the opening flap by not folding the triangle point in step 4.

Easy envelope

There are many ways to fold envelopes. This is one of the simplest and it is one of my creations. It only takes a few very simple steps, and the steps are relatively easy to remember, which makes it perfect for beginners. It takes almost no time at all to create this very useful envelope, which comes in handy when you can't find an envelope lying around the house when you need one. It can also be a letter fold – just fold your letter into this envelope shape. Use your favourite pretty paper to fold it because envelopes don't have to be boring. I like to add a little touch by decorating it with a small paper heart. You can find the heart place card instructions on page 40.

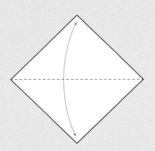

1. Fold the paper in half. Unfold.

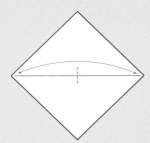

2. Fold the paper in half and make a small crease in the centre. Unfold.

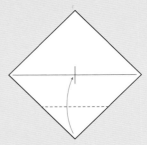

3. Fold the bottom point to the centre.

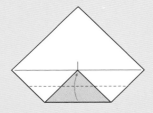

4. Fold the bottom edge to the centre.

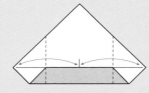

5. Fold the side points to the centre. Unfold.

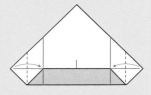

6. Fold the side points to the crease lines you just made.

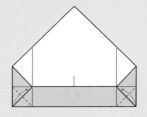

7. Fold the bottom corners up as shown.

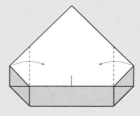

8. Fold the sides in on the crease lines from step 5 as shown.

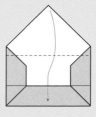

9. Fold the top down and tuck it into the pocket.

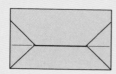

Your easy
envelope
is complete!

CREATE A HEART SEAL

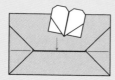

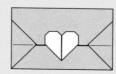

Easy envelope
with heart seal
complete!

Decorate the envelope by tucking a heart place card (see page 40) in the pocket. Use a piece of paper half the size you used for the envelope. For example, if you used a 15cm square piece of paper for the envelope, use a 7.5cm square piece for the heart.

Simple gift bag

This is probably the quickest, easiest and most clever way to fold a gift bag from a waterbomb base. Fold this from your favourite gift wrap and make it any size you want. You will never have to buy pre-made gift bags again! It can be self-closing if you follow step 9 precisely, otherwise you can close it with a ribbon or washi tape. This gift bag has a square base which makes it look cuter than the store-bought ones. It's a perfect little gift bag for party favours, wedding favours, party bags for kids or you can even use it to make an advent calendar!
Base used: waterbomb (page 21)

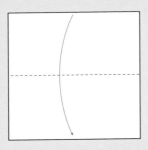

1　Fold the paper in half.

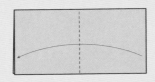

2　Fold the paper in half.

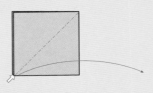

3　Lift the top layer and bring the corner to the right.

4　Line up the crease line and the centre, press down to flatten with a squash fold.

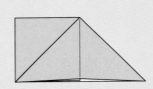

5　Turn over.

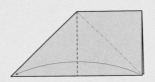

6　Lift the top layer and bring the corner to the left.

7　Line up the crease line and the centre, press down and squash fold into a waterbomb base.

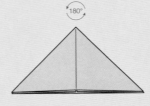

8　Rotate 180°.

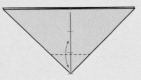

9　Fold the bottom point up just less than one-third of the way. Be precise if you want the gift bag to be self-closing. Unfold.

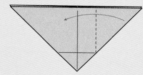

10 Fold the top right flap above the crease line you just made.

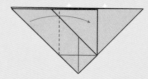

11 Fold the top left flap above the crease line you just made.

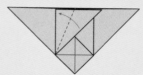

12 Fold the edge of the flap to the left, lining it up with the vertical edge.

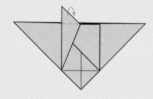

13 Fold the top triangle flap behind, over three layers of paper (the flap from step 10 and one layer of the bag).

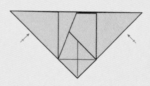

14 Repeat steps 10-13 on the other side.

15 Open the gift bag from the straight edge, and shape into a box.

Your simple gift bag is complete!

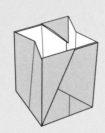

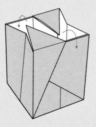

You can put a small present inside, and close by inserting the triangle flap between the first and second layers of paper on the opposite side. This only works if the crease line made in step 9 is precise enough.

Self-locking gift bag

This self-locking bag is one of my creations. The gift bag closes by tucking the opening flaps into one another. The top of the gift bag shows the reverse side of the paper, so consider using two-sided paper. To me, gift wrapping is as important as the gift itself. It's much more sentimental and thoughtful to use something you made, and the recipient will be impressed. When folded from a 15cm square piece of paper, this model fits a standard size lipstick perfectly. But of course, you can use it to wrap anything, just increase the paper size if you want to wrap something bigger.

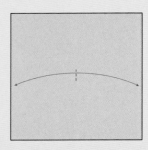

1. Fold the paper in half. Make a small crease on the dotted line in the centre as shown. Unfold.

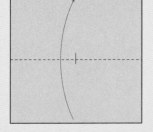

2. Fold the paper in half.

3. Divide equally into sixths. Fold the top edge down and the bottom edge up. Unfold.

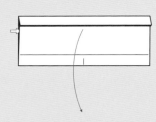

4. Open the paper. Make sure the top and bottom folds remain folded.

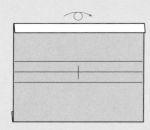

5. Turn over.

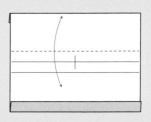

6. Refold the first crease line from the top to make it a valley fold line. Unfold.

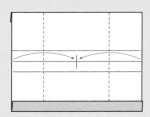

7. Fold both side edges to the centre.

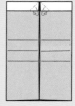

8. Fold the top inner corners back as shown.

9. Fold and unfold as shown.

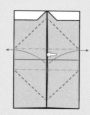

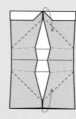

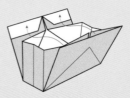

10 Open from the middle and bring the edges to the side.

11 Lift up the sides and bring the top and bottom edges to the centre a form into a rectangle-shaped box.

12 Tuck the top edge under the flaps of the opposite side to close.

Your self-locking gift bag is complete!

Menko pouch

I love this traditional menko pouch for its simplicity and elegance, and its interesting way of closing, which involves two layers. It is not completely flat so it is perfect to wrap small items in securely. It's important to get the mountain and valley fold lines correct, so when you push the paper in on all four sides (step 7) it will close like magic. Once you are familiar with the steps, you will find it therapeutic to fold. It makes a nifty gift pouch to wrap seeds in for plant lovers. If folded from bigger paper it can be used as a coaster. You could add weight to it by putting a piece of cardboard inside to make a paper toy called *ddakji*, similar to the one in the Netflix series *Squid Game*.

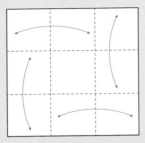

1 Fold the paper into thirds horizontally and vertically. Unfold.

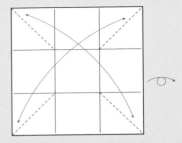

2 Fold diagonally and crease only the corner boxes as shown. Unfold and turn over.

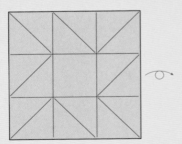

3 Bring the bottom corner to the red dot, crease only on the dotted line shown (middle box on the right side). Unfold.

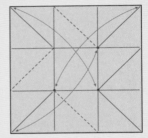

4 Repeat step 3 with the other three corners.

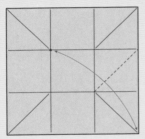

5 This is how the paper will look when all the crease lines are made. Turn over.

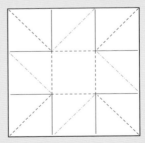

6 The crease lines you created now make mountain and valley folds.

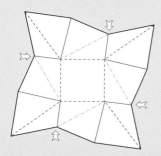

7   Slowly push the edges inwards at the tips of the mountain folds.

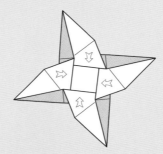

8   Continue to push the edges in, making sure the flaps overlap. Push down to close.

9   This is how it looks after closing.

10   Fold the left flap to the right.

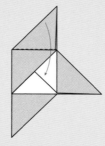

11   Fold the top flap down overlapping the left one.

12   Fold the right flap to the left.

Your menko pouch is complete!

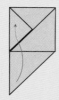

13   Fold the bottom flap up. Insert inside the pocket made by the left flap.

Index
of projects

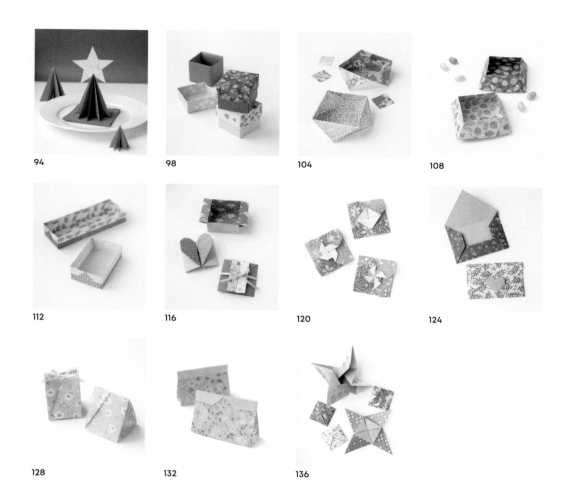

Suppliers

My favourite solid colour origami paper (known as kami paper) is made by Toyo. Kami paper is coloured on one side and white on the other. This paper is available on Amazon and from the Japan Centre (japancentre.com).

For origami paper with traditional Japanese motifs, I love the washi origami paper from Lavender Home (lavenderhome.co.uk).

For origami paper with cute patterns, my favourites are from Clairefontaine (clairefontaine.com).

I also like to shop for origami paper at Daiso Japan (daisojapan.com).

1

Published in 2023 by Ebury Press, an imprint of Ebury Publishing,
20 Vauxhall Bridge Road,
London, SW1V 2SA

Ebury Press is part of the Penguin Random House group of companies
whose addresses can be found at global.penguinrandomhouse.com

 Penguin
Random House
UK

First published by Ebury Press in 2023
www.penguin.co.uk

A CIP catalogue record for this book is available from the British Library.

Design: maru studio

ISBN: 9781529197648

Printed and bound in China

The authorised representative in the EEA is Penguin Random House Ireland,
Morrison Chambers, 32 Nassau Street, Dublin D02 YH68.

Penguin Random House is committed to a sustainable future for our
business, our readers and our planet. This book is made from Forest
Stewardship Council® certified paper.